BIRTHED REBIRTHED
AND BORN TURNED AROUND AGAIN

BIRTHED REBIRTHED
AND BORN TURNED AROUND AGAIN

Joseph Michael Shucraft

Foreword by Helmut Shucraft

RESOURCE *Publications* • Eugene, Oregon

BIRTHED REBIRTHED AND BORN TURNED AROUND AGAIN

Resource Publications
An Imprint of Wipf and Stock Publishers
199 W. 8th Ave., Suite 3
Eugene, OR 97401

www.wipfandstock.com

PAPERBACK ISBN: 978-1-6667-0598-0
HARDCOVER ISBN: 978-1-6667-0599-7
EBOOK ISBN: 978-1-6667-0600-0

06/15/21

I would Like to Dedicate this book to all those who have supported me. Friends, Church Family, Co-Workers, my home family, and all others not mentioned. May the blessings of Christ reign in your favor, and the sweetness of the sounds of rejoicing come for us all.

Sincerely,
Joseph Shucraft

CONTENTS

FOREWORD

I have watched Joe struggle with many things over the years. To me, this has been the sign of a very creative mind. I am a lyricist. So in a way, he has taken after me.

I must admit his work is much deeper and more introspective than mine. He achieves a much more colorful and enigmatic composition than I could ever hope to. His work is very thought-provoking and may give the reader their own epiphanies regarding life and their place in it. But that's just me. I welcome you to find out for yourself. Whether you read one at a time or the whole collection at once. I'm sure you'll understand for yourself the wonderful insights I have gotten from his poems and even cultivate a few of your own.

God Bless and Godspeed, Son

Your Dad Helmut Shucraft

PART I

SECTION I

New Day, New Beginning

Though I may walk through the valley of the shadow of disorder, I shall learn to speak naught to the evil one, hear it no longer, and profane not the name of Holiness, lest judgment come. I shall know to tell not any longer but the truth to the best of my knowledge. The Glory of the Lord is his almighty perfection, and he is wise in all his ways. No manner of evil will overcome God, the Father, who is ours. He will rise as the sun sets and falls, inevitably, as he has already arisen. Glory be to the Honor of God the Almighty, and Glory be to God the Glorious.

O', why would a prophet be disliked in their hometown? Surely he would not, if but truth will avail. Though I am not a prophet, I value their wisdom. A prophet may suffer at many times, perhaps being unheard and unheralded, but in the end, should he spread the truth, the Lord shall bless him. But he shall be faithful to his Prophets and bring them might in his name. His wisdom is his Holiness and divinity of his Grace. Speak and be good listeners; let the truth reign free. Love and it will come; the healing; with respect and kindness. Grace be to the Glory; as inevitably as the day sets, the sun will rise again tomorrow as you walk in the newness of life. In the name of Christ, Jesus, Amen.

Jesus, O' Peter, Rock of Christ

On this Church, bring salutations.
We are here and never shall fear.
Into the woods and to the plains
Brown, yellow, and gold
Though the ages have foretold
Men of great renown
Blessed be o' rock of God
Foundation of the world
Sinners o' to repent
The end of the era, the coming of the night
Where shall we hide and go
The arrival of the light
Of which were and of who
Shall I go to be?
How shall I be raised, and to where shall I be?
To whom shall I come, wherefore shall I go?
Who it was and shall always be?
There was not but love in their hearts?
How did we go astray?
It hurts the pain that has become,
The love of God is always faithful and shall be yours if you believe.
The coming of the night
Delivers us into his hands

You Are

You are the fill for the emptiness.
You are the giver of true happiness.
Mercy by your name
Glory by your honor
Holiness by your presence
Divinity in your truth
Tenderness in your love
Spirit in your touch
Graciousness in your halls
Light in the darkness
Strength in the weak

Brood

Castaway of disorder, dismay as you may
You may love and become like him someday.
Here and let it be known.
I love you, my friend
Do not believe the lies of the Devil.
Evil as they are
Though they are there, he is there as well.
Jesus will save you from sin.

Devil Is in The Night

My dreams are a terror, not a melody.
Children screaming a hapless memory.
Screaming out for love from above
It is the Devil in the night.
Prayers to the God above
Waiting for the first star in the sky
To lead me to my home.

A horror show blackens my eyelids.
I see a little bit of the evil.
All that the Devil could bring,
He brought it to me in the middle of my sleep.
It is the Devil in the night.
Prayers to the God above
Waiting for the first star in the sky
To lead me to my home.
It is Heaven in the dawn of day.
God in the clouds above
I see his plan for me.
Above all, my worst dreams.
Because
It is the Devil in the night.
Prayers to the God above
For his peace, his mercy, and his love

He Saves Us

Here I never knew
Always saw, but never came true.
A dream of restless wind
And of dying seasons.

I spot adrift near the horizon.
I am running nearer
I am always falling
I flipped that around.
Turned it upside down
My head filled
I am lifeless

I wake up to you
You were there when I fell.
You took me from my hell.
With you, I flew to Heaven.

Jesus only knows why
I am let in
He drew me away from my sin.
He took me torn
He took me after the fall.
He sent me up to Zion.

The Lion always sees
The King of the Jungle is roaring.
Always on the hunt for souls
Saving where you are standing

His grace is without a match.
He delivers the troubled out of the cold.

He warms them with his love.
He takes us in, and he clothes us.

Jesus frees us from our sins.
His cross to bear the burden
His wounds and his scars
Are not our own

Brother Shed a Tear

There is a flame on the horizon and a simple shutter in the wind.
A twain of mockery and faint discomfort stuck between the two.
Burdensome though, the self-disdain, it will get better in the end

Brother shed a tear
Let the flame dim, and the wind die down.
Brother makes it clear.
Mock the mocker and scorn the Devil
Brother, let us get here.
Free ourselves so we can stop and help each other It is Jesus' last stand that
brings us home.

Troubles of two begotten unto one is a separation from prosperity.
The identity of self apart from others is not a sanctuary of mind.
Delusion is the problem and the cause born from ill knowledge.

Brother shed a tear
Lay it all bare and let your strife lay barren
Brother, make it clear.
Come clean and open to the Lord.
Brother, let us get here.
Cast away Abaddon
Let Jesus take the throne.

Freedom

Moving without strife
Burdens lifted, the almighty ease.
Troubles dissolving, resolutions becoming entwined
The decadence surrounding us and filling up our minds
Like a mighty mountain birthing a flowing river
Giving us renewal in a sumptuous stream

The high and mighty river of life flowing from the tree thereof
Giving us providence, the divine inspiration
Creating us from dust till dust we do settle
Designed for purpose and instructed with mettle

Through Trial and Order
Discomfort and Distain
His prophets give us the knowledge we do gain.
To overcome evils wherefore, they beseech our dismay.

Power of the almighty, freedom from transgression
Your anger, your hate will be cast with your sins.
To a bottomless pit with haste and due care
So, tarry you not, come to the Lord.
Your freedom is here within

Forgiveness

It is not just for you.
Or just for me
It is for everybody
It is a relief

Forgiveness
For your wrongs and trespasses
For a better world and a free mind
Taking us from the bottom to the top
And taking the top to the bottom.

Some things cannot be changed.
Songs unsung
Boasts canceled
Trials cast, and burdens placed.
But healing can take shape.

Forgiveness
It is what Jesus taught.
Forgiveness
It is why Jesus fought.
Forgiven
So, deny it naught
For Christ died, so you might live.

He's There Without You

Where were you?
When I felt all the pain
Where were you?
Were you hiding in your solace?
Were you running from my side?

While I was in my misery
There was no one to be found.
Not even one to care
Or so I thought
Until he came to save me
To take me to the light.
To calm the stormy night.

He was there
With nobody else to be found
When I hit my head and fell
When my shame covered my pride
He was there, by my side.

He took me from my ache.
Filled my cup and blessed me so
Picked me up, a lonely vessel.
Stopped all the terror of the dark
Star of Bethlehem, O' Holy Night

I prayed, o' God, thank you for your Son.
I am lost without and now am found.
Down and out, but becoming strong
With His Word, I Am Healed
His Blessings that Shall Grace All Who Bear His Name
That Grace that is Perfection

Perfection through his Blood
The Salvation, Redemption proceeding from it

When I hurt, I remember him.
When
I am in the fire; I am protected.
And through the sacrifice, it brought eternal life.
As I go into the shadows of despair
I take God as my light
His burden to bear for me

As we walk through the land together, we shall rejoice.
For he has found you, my friend.
And though you hid for a while
You were never lost
For if he sees all
Then where could you go?

I see you are hurting too.
A bandage and limp
On your last leg, wondering, why?
Pleading for an answer
You must but listen and go.
He shall lead, and you follow.
Let Heaven take you home.

Frosty Meadows

You tested
Trial and order
Restoration and virtue
Might and meek
Chaos and enlightenment

The storehouses of God shall descend like a mighty wind.
The planting of the trees shall usurp the meadows.
The grinding of the mill shall press the vine of the wicked.
The dark shall not see the light, but the light shall forestall the darkness.
In the light shall be salvation.
In the darkness chaos

When the Judging of the Nations comes, and the children counted.
Where will you stand
Will you be a Child of the light?
Or let darkness take its stance?

I Wish I Could

I wish I could wake up with you around.
But I was dead to the head, and I did not even know what was going on.
I hurt and took it all out on what I love.
Beauty is all I see
I could be happy if I only had not hurt so much.
I just wanted my fantasy to come true.
If it could be you and me, I would make it so
I was dead in the head; you made it better.
You do not know, but I saw something, and I was happy.
For the first time in a long time
I started to hear for the first time in my life.
It hurts to know that I could not figure out what was happening.
I was frightened, and my pain was blackened.
Threatened by people in my guise and deeply saddened
Why do they lie about me before I get a chance?
Do I hear the voices as they dance?
I hate it when they deal with me in advance.
I hope they choke out of it for all its caused
All I want is love

In the Wind

Rushing through the waves of the running field
Dancing over the dawn to the last of the fleeting embrace
Turning through the shadow casting out the darkness
The void is calling through the running of the plains.
Shall I arise in the coming of the dawn?
While I become a shadow or brook of the field
Shall I emerge and run or catch the light of the ray?

Or the sun of the rain and the wind of the valley
Shall it grow the light?
Shall I bear my fruits and render thee asunder?
Shall I be reborn in the truth and the light?
Right as I might say as I shall do
Praise today and a night over the land.
The view of the Lord through the fields and the rain
The message of God will grow with peace and with might.
Shall I lead to the strength of the almighty and the braveness
of the heavens?
The Garden is growing, and the age is turning.
Experience the healing of the era through the rock of the night
Racing through the river and riding the winds and the rain
The harvest shall be ripe, and the seed shall show through you
all; it will grow.
The might of the hammer the grandeur of splendor
His elegance shall rain through the mountains; rivers shall flow, fertile
shall be the land.
I would tell you more, as only I shall listen through fire and mortar,
iron, and steel.
Arise sons and daughters through the rock and the fire
Slain by the Spirit of the Lamb who was slain
Through fire and rain, toil, and hardship
Matters of mercy to be attended to through the rock of delight

The brain of the subject through an organ and a slight
The Lamb shall arise, the one who was slain.
The Spirit of God plain as through the eyes of the rain
When shall we see and do, right?
Shalt it naught blessed by the cup of the storm of the Lamb.
Blessed be the peacemaker, the signer of the treaty through might.
Shall we all run to gather the round of the bright
Shall it be around to the end of the day?
Right nor wrong to the end of the day and through the blessings of the fire
The patter weaves as the bright blossom shall reign inundated.
Prism of God Lord of the rain do naught disdain.
Shall it be a thousand or more, how long shall he reign
Through the deep of the depths, the depth of the deep
Running through the shadow and tearing it down.
Shall it rise, shall it dwell down
Rise o' sun of the Son, the one of only the only of one
Run around the round of the ripe
The Tree of Life shall arise.
With knowledge shall it go forth, but where shall it go.
Tree of the run bathed in the sun
Grown and growing, tattered, and torn
Read through to the shadow of it all.
Ripen with fruit; blessings shall arise.
The running of the till
The riding of the storm
As I shall appear slain by the Spirit
Running through the wild, the brush of the sage.
See and do know, run, and do wander.
Run through the way and seek o' the fortune
Bought not of fame, picked not of the run.
The flaming sword of the risen of the rise.
Run to the written, the word of The Tree of Life
Should I run and hide or wander for a time.
The run, the ride, the weather through and through
As I shall rise and rise, I shall be burning one o' burning one.
Shall the bush be of fire, and shall I listen, o' listen?
How many visions, how many divines, seer o' the celestial sea
Runner of the rain of the Lamb that was slain

Sacrifice o' toil run and till many a year for the field of the light
Till the toil, run and circle the land.
Rider o'er the sun, child of the light
Tongue flaming as the sword
Steal the seal and run onward
Freely run and run, toil the land.
Arise through the ashes and dot the eye of the cheek through the way
Fold of the Earth; Lion arises to rest and rest to arise.
Baptized in fire and mortar
There is no rest for the presumptuous as they run around, and
they heap burdens.
Run through and see the light, the man of the land and the leader of might
Runner, o' runner, toil and delight, trouble not through the sea
of the ill will
Holy Spirit of the Lamb that was slain
I run far away and through the ash.
Bringer of death trouble, not the land
Rain pure and the goods of the land
Through mirth and might of steel and the army
Strength through the toiler and runner through the gray
Bend in the shadow of the area of the free cover o' the rock from the sun
Boulder for bold reign or the sun
Runner of the band, the clan of the man
Shall I arise and run through the land, and shall I slow to hold a hand?
Peace be upon you through the rise of the grain runner of the mighty.
Arise o' Messiah bringer of the light
Through sackcloth and sandalwood
Son of the God
God of the Sun
Reign of the Peace
Maker of the Valley
Run through the Majesty
Might through the Valley
Rusher o' so slow
Looking for a love God reaps, and so shall he sow
Little of light
Peacemaker, no death shall you see.
You shall arise of the majesty, might of it all.

Run, o' Lord, fleet to the might of the rain, let it trouble us
naught without gain.
Rain o'er the land blessed o' healer.
Rainmaker, sun lighter
. Rock o' the mighty area of the rain
Peace be upon you o' Lord of the main.
Reign o'er the land
Peacekeeper
Bringer of light

Innocent

What would you say when you were young?
Where would dreams take you?
How would you know what to do?
Hiding in your chamber fearful of the World

This world can be inundating.
You must find your way.
But, without a means, roughhewn is where you will stay.
Afraid of what you could be
Scared of who you are
Wanting to change
But change is always so far.

Cast off from reality
You stumble and fall.
No end in sight
To this ceaseless fight

Going to battle without a weapon
No armor to bear
Let it not keep you down.
It is time for you to share
Be lifted by his grace.

He sends his Son to take your place in suffering.
So why do you still suffer?
Though he is there, he wants others like you to help.
To bring each other together and to know where you each are from
Together we are stronger.
An army and a tribe of believers

It takes a village to raise a village,

Not only half but the whole tribe
Do not forsake each other, or you will never reach your goal.
Of truth, surely, prosperity is made.

Do not deny what is inside.
You never run away
From whom you are, and where you have been
It is your life that is swaying.

The clock turns, and we all die someday.
So, will we take each chance and make a better stay?
Here on God's green Earth
Where your debt is paid accordingly by God
Washed away

SECTION II

Lonely

Left beside on a wayward path
Taken advantage of and used
A beaten man who knows only wrath
Alone and afraid, not seeing a way to get to the promised land

Stumbling in my terror, not knowing a real place
Where I can stand and look in the mirror
And not see a troubled face.
I call to the night, are you there?

Are you something I can see or something I can feel?
When I run, will I find my home?
Where can I go to find myself someplace real?
Should I hide from you, or should I tell the truth?

In my memories, I search to find your peace.
In them, I find love, something I thought I never felt.
You brought an end to this terror, the fight that indeed did cease.
And in your name, it was cast aside, the falseness of the lies.

You would have to understand
What it truly is and why it came to be
It comes without a blind reprimand.
He knows who you indeed are

Jesus knows when you have gone astray, for how long and how far.
Where you are going and when you will get there
It is because he is our shining star.
When I take the wrong path, he is the guide back to what is right.

Though I hurt, it is at an end.
With the love of Yahweh in my grasp
His love that genuinely does mend
Strengthens me and supports me so I can be a better man

Muddy Waters

I was running away, little did I see
Blind and burdened, I could not be put at ease.
Where I was going, no direction in me.
My faith was shattered, and peace not there.

I was hurting; many did care.
Until Jesus came and stood by my side
He put the mud in my eyes.
Washed clean, it was then I find
The Lord healed me of that, I am sure.
All of you he welcomes too
People stood in line and all to say
Jesus is the only way.

Prayers answered, and the Lord praised
The people shouted, "It can only be God's grace."
That healed this Son.
Made it so he can be someone

New Day

Today is another day after the other.
A new way to pray for forgiveness pleading on your knees
When this life hits the floor, and I just want to end this pain.
That is when I feel it again.

Today is a New Day
Not at all like last Monday
One more day next to Sunday
There is nothing like his Spirit to make me beam.
Today is a New Day

I have praise for my soul today.
I feel a little less broken, and I am okay.
My shattered appearance is restoring.
In the presence of the Lord, I say

Today is a New Day
One not at all like the rest of my days
More healing, feeling less ashamed.
Jesus houses the weary.
Restores us to righteousness
Today is a New Day

Outstretched Arms

My face
Sunken deep
I cannot pass
Without first to leap

Outstretched arms can feel heavy.
When held for so long
I always hurt; I never see the reason why

Then came lightning and thunder.
It struck me where I am
It made me a different man.

Once deaf and mute
Now I sing on borrowed time.
Never in my life would, I think.
That I could be strong
Or capable of anything but wrong

My time is short
Quicksand would make it longer.
My heart is stopping now.
If I could prolong it somehow.

I would tell you all that I love you.
I am sorry for all my problems.
I did not mean for them to be yours.
I want you to know
That you are truly loved

Here, my last moments flashing by.
No tears for me, I hope.

I do not want you to feel my pain.
No one should go where I am surely going.
I know that I am not worthy.
Surely not without sorrow
Waiting for God's call to end this 'morrow

Roads

On this journey
A path down a road
On that road is a fork.
A decision to be made

Left or Right
East or West
Truth or Not
Friend or Foe

Sometimes I feel like I do not have a choice.
That evil is all this body can reap
An utterance that is not from me
I never want to see it again.
The evil and its ugly twin

When I run, I see him follow.
When I hide, he seeks.
And in the darkness, he finds me.
I do not know him as my father.
Only as the desolate one
Creeper of the deep

So, I choose to stand and fight.
I use the shield of faith.
My body is weak
Mind weary

But with the full armor of God at my disposal.
Satan is no match
A simple lie cannot defeat our God
When deceit be your ungainful end

Your slip fold sours.
Truth will abound
In time, the darkness will quell
The binder will reap and be bound.
The serpent, as you call him, shall fall.
His tongue shall go numb.
Shame will subdue him to his prison.
God, the bearer of light and his mighty scepter shall reign.
The Kingdom of Heaven, the almighty rule
And the river of living water vast.
There is room for all that claim the blood of the Lamb and
ride bearing truth.
When you think you have nothing, do try to remember.
The riches of Heaven can be yours if you endure.

When I fall, withered, stained with blood.
Will I rise again?
Will I be cast aside like a wastrel?
A loud cry against the deceit

As my Savior lives
So, shall I
As I weep
Him as well
The angels rejoice
When we escape from Hell
The bark of the hounds will be far from the gates.
The song of the damned will seals their fates.
When they lie, cheat, blaspheme, and murder, it increases
their wickedness.
So, it is with due haste we must rise and conquer our foe.
The Devil, the evil, the sin of the world
Seal them in their prison
In fire and mortar
Sealing misdeeds
Forever

Shine in the Rainbow

Thrice of old
Triple score three
Twenty out nine
Seventy-three times seventy-nine
I hit the green on the sidewalk.
Little shy in the light
Walk around
With a channel in my hand
Wondering why we go through this man
Dreams of butter and sugar and cream
Cropping up daisies and pushing lilies
Working the field and picking the fruit
Dead to the Earth and picking the dirt
Green and the red
Sober and sour
Orange of the sun
Green of the Labor
Tree of Life
Crop of Renown
We have come to the point where the lost find themselves.
You know where I am; you know where they are
Where drowning out the tune of the hour
What do we offend when we do not work together?
United, we fall when together we do not stand.
When commanded by him, where will you go?
Unto the furnace or over the show
If you are hurting, it is clear
We all must reach to the world at mass with a cherubim's staff.
O' green of leaf, take the tower of Babel
Beat the 'roundabout and run all around
Take the good old son of the Lamb that was slain.
Wear our badge on our chest and not get left for last

To the table, we will go, together we breathe.
Hurting no longer
Together we sing
Green and the red
Sober and sour
Orange of the sun
Green of the Labor
Tree of life
Crop of Renown

Something Pretty

So, you say you are something saintly.
Rapture only knows, and I cannot tell.
When you go by, the saints are weeping.
Half a mind to see where you are going
So, the direction can be changed and save you from perdition.

So, you say your something pretty.
You look down on me, and you think you know.
Something pretty cannot be so malevolent.
Hate cannot free you from your prison.

So, you say you are beautiful.
You also think a fiend is not unwelcoming.
You make your pacts for emulsions and pastels.
Oh, you think you are so attractive, though not as you would appear.
Cannot even tell bliss from perdition

So, you say you are honest.
You do not even know who pays your fliers.
Writing checks to only the finest of confinements.
Mocking but the God above

Holiness be upon you and make you pretty.
Your distaste for yourself keeps you going.
You think without having been confronted too often.
Not the sufferer in the pit where you feel you belong

I pray to Jesus, come, and save you.
Turn this one into a beauty.
Save their soul and bury their disdain.
Teach them to love like you taught me

Once I thought I was attractive.
Thought I could do as I thought as well
Once I thought I was above it.
The good Lord told me that's profanity.

So, you think you are attractive.
God sees you as he saw me.
He will make you beautiful.
He will put your burdens at ease.

You do not feel pretty.
Just dolled up, hurting inside.
Looking for another out
You have got something to hide.

Let it out and lay it bare.
I know you know you are not pretty.
Deep inside, you do not feel like you are worth much.
God knows your pain
God will make you beautiful again.

Soul, Mind, Body, Spirit

Soul, mind, body
All are a part of what makes me who I am
My soul is weak, and you bring it restoration.
Mind bent and all distorted

I seek your wisdom
Do to me as you will
All I ask is that my mind should set on you.
And the ways of your perfection.
Take me to a place of heavenly bliss.

Lull me to sleep
Rock the cradle and make me deeper
I am wondering when I will awaken in your arms.
And you will tell me how much I mean.
You will say to me tales of why and how
I will know life's true meaning.

My body contorted
I have no will to go on.
I hear you now but only nearly.
When I see you, I am happily dreaming.
Of the day you first came into my life.

The day was long, and I was far away.
Coming near, though cast astray
I humbly bent and bowed.
I cried aloud, and you heard me then.
Said, "I love you," and your arms were open.
Welcoming me into a walk of faith
The faith that grace gives was all that is needed.

My promise, as meager as could be
Is that I will remember all you did for me
When the wind blows, and the chill follows.
Your warmth surrounds me.
My soul, mind, and body
Enveloped by your Spirit

SECTION III

Stranger

You hear me now, and I am not familiar.
Not from here where you all know each other
I am a different man than you are used to
The kind you do not like, nor care if I am something

You hear my cries, but with only deaf ears.
You do not like that I am a broken, crumpled leaf in the wind.
My worst sin is that you will not hear me.
You do not care, and you do not know me.
Where I have been and who loves me
Only God could tell

You think you are perfect in your anger.
Thinking destined for a downward bent prison
Life's ordinate dishevelment
You wish you could know.
What it would take to get me there sooner.

You should not stare at this sinner.
It is not polite, and you have never been nearby.
Have not had these succubae
Lost in the clear

Never been bit by the serpent.
Only been touched by the crooked ways.
So, you say to me
You are a sinner, a wretch; you shall not enter.
Go back to the pit where you belong.

So, you think you know where I am going.
Well, I say I will fight the touch.
Will not give in and let it take me
Fight this sin and shed my sorrows.

I will not forget my vile, an antidote.
You fight and say it is genuinely poison I am taking in.
You want me to keep going down the wrong path.
But I know who loves me the most.

The Lord our God, a Shepard
Part of the flock he is undoubtedly tending
He has got nail wounds for you and me.
Do not deny why he died; just love and cry.
When you hear me now, will you open your ears?
Tell a friend and swallow your gallantry.
Tried and true Christ is the only compass.

Yours only points north.
If that is what you say, you are lying.
You, like I many a time, am guilty of sending yourself below your
actual position.
Think your fury is only just
You are lying to yourself.
If the only way you can win is beating down the troubled
Then when will you ever get a real gain?

If you feel pain, it is only natural.
Hurting friend, welcome to living.
Life's an altruistic version of death.
Until our leader conquered our fiends
Sent them far into their anguish
Punished them because they are the source of our problems
Not all on us, we must ponder.
That sometimes we can be stricken.
Dumped on by the defectors to God

They run loose, and we get trampled.

Without him, we never can become whole.
Now you know you are a sinner.
Not the only one in a lifetime
The boat is full, and you never know who is aboard.
Armageddon is not the end but a beginning.
The last stand of the faithful and mighty
You may think I am a sinner.
Fact is, I know I am, but God's not done with me yet, not this wretch.
I know he will fix me.
I might not be a mighty warrior.
A leader in the army of men
But the Son of God will still behold me.
Into the army of Heaven above

You see, he does not use only the perfect.
There are none but him.
So, shed your false honor.
Quit acting as though you are the only might of the worthy
You are callous without redemption.
Think nothing terrible could happen
Never been where he has been or where I am going.
The fact is that Christ's last stand will have us all coming home.
So, praise the God above for his love.
I will race you to the gates if you can stand.
To stand in line with the blood of the Lamb.

To My Father's

It is time to go away from here.
Wherever I am headed, I hope you will find me.
When I cried, I heard you calling.
In the distance, a spirit voice distinctly saying.
"My life is yours, and yours is to be mine."

Will you set me free?
Will I find new meaning?
And find peace in your calling.
Knowing that I rest and pray
Today I find that you love me.

It is not a broken promise or a false messiah.
It is a truth on that of which I lean.
The fact that you will save me
When I am lost, I know I have been found.

It is a shadow in the wind.
That wakes me where I am
Takes me to where I am going

I am a wanderer, a loner, and a sinner.
A cold and broken piece of clay
Dried and in a rut, living day today
Wondering when my time will come
When will you take me to where I should be?

Waiting to be more than just another broken vessel
Hearing all the praises of your love
I sit and think
Will you heal me?

Will you take that clay and make it useful?
Will you mold me in the image of a real man?
I could be like the prophets someday if you made me.
I could preach the word if the word were yours.
I could spread your love if I had it myself.

Within my reach, I see the valley.
The mountains that are the highest
It is a long climb if you are willing.
Jesus is at the top, waiting for you sinners.

He is teaching the good news to the poor.
Spreading love to the meek and mild
And teaching others like me to get better.
He loves you where you are at and where you are going.

He is here to point you in the right direction.
Step into the light and shed your burden
When you lie down for the night at your Father's house,
Will you remember to give him thanks for his giving Spirit?
The nights were cold until I got here.
The days were long, and so I bought it.
Peace to me now and a restful midnight
It is a loving light that brings us home.

To Rest for A Day

To rest today, tomorrow and eve.
Today an hour, tomorrow shall sour.
I think, this day, that a snow shall fall.
Tomorrow, wherefore shall I be
Shall I ride in the north 'till the plains do roam
Another ride for a season, a plain or rhyme or reason
Today I shall find a sign in the clear blue sky.
For a rain, a time beside the hay.

I run freely uncaged as I see you running in the bay.
Wherever they shall roam, let them be merry and blessed.
Worthy are they that make peace.
Blessed are those that love and, today, those that gather.
I love each day, one another, side by side; alone I ride.
Another day, I'm lost another day I find a way to rest 'till I stay.
It is a little bit colder, and I am slowly fading away.

I just want to say, "Hi," and hear you say, "I love you."
Peace upon you is all I say

To the World Where I Am

Where did I run? Where am I going?
Went down to where I am hiding again
Lost in the desert, I am wandering.
Down to my last, I am a lonely one.

Where will I go when I am made new?
Where will I go when I come to know you?
Will I hide from the one, and who will beseech you?
I am tired of playing this game because I am lost again.

My only one and real lonely secret
The one and only one I ever knew
There is one inspiration I keep on my mind.
It takes a world for me to be on this side.

Here I am found in this moment.
This one time, I am getting shone on by the sun.
Found a way to reconnect to my true nature
The beauty resting in the sun

I love it when you rest and hold me.
Beauty of the winds and the true Spirit
I find my way home when I am around you.
I am tired of being lonely.
Tired of being split in the wind of my own sundry

I am a lover, and I am tired of fighting to be me.
Who am I without knowing that you love me?
Here I am, and I am lost again.
In the wintertime
Wishing for the weather to turn me in the right direction
I love it when I am running and become found again.

Basking in the round of the wheat that meets the barley
Smoked

SECTION IV

Truth of the Breath of Death to The Truth of the Way of Life and Spirit

Run upon the ground
Disk through the air
Eating the torso of the rest of the pair.
Flying through the clouds
Higher than the sun
Render it as asunder
With the rest of you, there
I heard the calling of the flight through the foreyard.
The last blast of the plague
Kindling the plow of the end of the age
Death to the Death
End of decay
End of the ages
The end of dismay
Valley of the feet
Mountain of the basket
Filler of the feed and might of the rapids
Hear it roar and let it soar
It shall come and lend and tomorrow rend.
Reaping of the Earth, the plight of the blight
It hath come, and the rest have gone.
Building of the plenty and the plenty of the young
May there might have a fold, and the plenty told.
May you all be blessed, and your day be merry.
Whether you have wheat or whether you have terry
Follow us now, and you shall feed
Do not lend low, or you shall not be reborn.
The newness of life is yours if we keep it together.

Truth of salvation is the creed of the might and the death to the blight.
Carry a swift wit and a true sword sharpened well to the dull day.
Do not use the departure from the metal to end without love
Pain in life is an end to suffering.
Love cures evil
Evils from suffering do not impart pain, but strength is impart-
ed in overcoming.
Feeling pain from suffering is to understand hardship.
And overcoming the fight and set up a fortress of might.
It takes a swift wit.
Tact
And a healer's touch.
With a rhythm and beat
Touch and sound
Beat it and defeat
Then end of the plague.

What Jesus Said

What he did, lives in me; it is not dying but breathing like he is
He comforts me when I am crying because he bled the way he did
I am not perfect, though I am trying and seeking purpose through living.

What Jesus said inspires me to be born again.
What Jesus said teaches me to learn to love instead.
What Jesus said keeps me from thought of deadly sin.
If it is what he does for me, he does it for you too.

I have a hole that wrought within my being.
Trying my life and giving me a grotesque feeling.
Pain escapes me daily as burdened with life's folly.
Trial is my twin, and twist of thought, my enemy.

What Jesus said feels right, just like what he did.
What Jesus said fills me with his pure Spirit.
What Jesus said is a never-ending truth.
If I feel at wit's end, he keeps me from the edge.

Why o' Me

Turned all about
Sat and ran a spun
Grazed and unknown
Below, but up high
All, but none

Cast astray
Wishing to be underneath the grip
O' my soul is weak
Tried down, never tied down, just slain about round the side
Hurting all day, no joy, I wish to be happy.

Bright and morning star
How have you fallen afar?
Pain comes to the deepest of nights, shining bright in the big yellow dwarf.
I am aching; I am burning cannot seem to settle down.

Eating a whole, a whole new meaning, timber cast on down.
Where will I go from here?
Where will you send me?
How do I become what you want me to be?
Will I survive the gambit and receive a new life?

When gourds ring, shall the people sing
Holy one
When will you find some love?
When will you be blessed and receive our kind?
Where shall we go from here?
Will you hold us, dear?
Keep us in our prayers every day.

O' Lord, it ever aches not to ease this pain

Send us your mercy, blessed by the Lamb of our God.
Be it not by wrath
Heal us our lands and save us in your arms.

Bless your seats of power
May they grow ever stronger
As you fill us up
Never looking down again

Meet in the center
Holding the Branch of Peace
Making pacts with love
Ever ending 'naught
Bleeding in the light of the day

May the wind spin slow
May all you grow
As spirit flows and you sow Godly desires
Bring me the altar
Call me to the choir.

Enjoy bliss and joy
True happiness
Do not fight the light.
Join in the march of God
Let Heaven conquer from above to below.

Heal us with your glory.
Grace us with the might that is yours, God
Surround us in undying blessings
Pick me up and lift me to your throne.
Send me to where you go.
Lead, and we follow
Holy One, the bringer of the end of our pain

God bless the mercy and mercy bestowed by God unmatched.

Windows and Widows

Does the orphan child have a name?
Does the widow know she was once a bride?
Does God know I exist?

In this World, we create as if there is no consequence.
A widow we make
Where there is bondservant
Tomorrow we take the master.
When there is no bride for the groom
There is no groom
Blind eye for matching tooth

The grinding of the wheel turns, and there is no loom.
No thread bearing needle

Without clothes, aren't we but naked?
Without food starving
Without God nothing

When we take ourselves and gaze upon ourselves?
Will we see as God does?
Or will we see as the mad King?
God of oblivion
Caster of shadows
Deceiver of Nations
Father of lies
Destroyer
Will the cock crow thrice, and we become counted?
And counted to where?
Will we be like Peter?
Or will we be like Daniel?
Will, we become as the Lion,

And the Lamb?
Will the Son of God be our rest?
Will we bear our iniquity?
Will you hear me, now?

Does God know we exist?
In existence is God
God is existence
Embrace him; we must

For when we are laid low down and in pieces
Who picks them up?
Who tills the field when we cannot?
Does not the fool get cast aside for when they cannot bear?
Do we deserve it?

When we are but children, and we can feel the very presence of God
When we are adults, are we still not but children to God

What is eternity, but a fleeting moment in the eyes of God
When some second passes to us
To God, many years follow.

Is it gold you seek?
Does fortune favor the wise?
Do the wicked take that which belongs not to them?
Is there justice in the end?
Does it hurt to die?

Surrounded in the valley are lily's you say
Do they look beautiful like you?
Or do they wither and die like me?

I am but a fisherman, lost at the heavenly sea.
With no lighthouse
No mooring lines
Wishing for even a deserted plane
Anything but the drowning that is to come

Will I burn in hellfire?
Will I be redeemed?
Did I not seek first the Kingdom of God?

Did I not do a respectable job?
Did they listen?
Did they hear?
Are they coming with me?

Is it the depths of the abyss?
Or the mire of fog
Maybe it is the Light of the Lord our God.

I think I see it coming on the horizon.
I think I see God's bliss.

Your Maker

When you meet your maker
With your soul to bear
Will you remember me?
Will I remember you?

When you meet your maker
Will you be caught up with him?
Will you be tangled with your sin?
Your life, yours, only nothing valued

Will you run to his arms?
Or turn your head and fall.
With God, always there.
And your tears run dry.

Do you think I will be there?
Or will I be downstairs?
With the torturer
And the scarecrows of my life.

Will I run away?
Just turn my head and cry.
With lust all gone
And my fears end in sight.

Will you run to his arms?
Or turn your head and fall.
With God, always there.
And your life in his arms.

Will the river flow
Next to the Tree of Life?

To Me from Him

Have faith, my Son
All will be well
I am healing as we speak.
Rest when you are weary
Walk when you are able.
Keep on going
Fear not, for the Lord thy God loves you
He feeds you when you are weary.
Rests and prays
Ask not the Lord for forgiveness without having sought it yourself.
Forgive, and you shall have forgiveness.
If a man slaps, you then turn the other cheek.
If it is so, then let it be
Heal me o' God
Savior of my people
Speak, and be it given to you should your intentions be noble.
Ask, and it shall come.
But be diligent and do not ask for more than you can handle at once

SECTION V

Power and Love

Firth and fire, meek and mild
Love from sinner reconciled.
Meek and mountain, firth, and fountain
Following yonder star
Peace
Yonder star
Wonder fountain, follow you.
Submissive oh mountain glory, and spray, following yonder star
O' order for beauty, mercy reign, love and wonder
Following yonder star
Strife be naught, o' weary might.
Love and bliss, holy and miss
How did I wander far?
Before I found you and your love
Wandered wander, traveled o' so far
Till I find my holly bliss
Traveling, I wandered afar.

Brightness of Our Peace and Love

Following from over in the distance and wondering from and far
Mercy might and take our flight.
Fly, o' far off, the night.
Where, o' where, o' where do you see
How o' did you see me o' me?
Where did you find the bliss?
Merry lot o' merry loft and cherry underneath the lime of light
We follow all that is bright.
Glory, what is it naught
Naught, but o Lord, o' please follow the yonder star

That and To You the End of The Night

When o' when will it end?
The verse, the script, the story, the bend?
When shall I cry, when shall I mend?
Where do I go to turn around and reach the lent?
How do I wander, o' so, and how so far?
It hurts quite a lot to walk through and to so far.
It hurts, the pain, and the bright morning mend.
Running around and hurting, never knowing when?
Flowing from around, where will you go, and how will I be found?
When will I run, and where will I go?
Do the brave triumph through the pain?

When will I roam, and where?
Does it hurt to triumph from mercy?
You understand where the shadows loom but do not see the rain
over the cloud.
Precisely where should it be when it is placed upon the
frown of the storm?
The green rain of the rock stems from the end of the round.
There are twenty steps from a turn to a corner around the way.
From the Tree of Life

See the low and behold
How does it take away to around?
This end of night shall come around twice and once more thrice.

To the Day

Day or night, sign, or sorrow
Flying free about looking for a day
Some way just to say what I mean.
It is bliss when I see what you think of me.
How does it hurt to feel life without you?
Without a flag to fly above the sky in the plains
Cutting a bit more until shattered
Somehow, I do not understand why we cannot meet.

Who shall find me when I wake from my bed?
Shall I meet you, or be it death instead?
When I wander in the agora, I will be on the look.
Looking for one with such grace, elegance, tact, and love
I do not seek, but the love of the peace meant for you.
To see you in pain would cause me to ache in your stead.
Without the hurt in my eyes, I would not know what to do.
Sadness has become instilled in me.
I have become begotten unto woe.

Fill me up

I am drained

I do not know why I cannot breathe without a hacking noose.

I cannot see without stumbling in your presence.

I see you coming in the clear.

Riding in on the way from and for me

It is coming, the healing you have told me to believe in

This end to the death of my spirit

To be filled with the enlightenment of your knowledge is the
only way to live.

By your word, do we gain the truth of existence?

In your presence, does the power multiply.

May the grace and glory of God be upon you.

I shall rest in the knowledge that my journey has brought me home.

I shall no longer linger at the table but instead go to the altar.

There I shall call out your name.

Together forever, we shall fight.

Pretend

How do I pretend I do not know what I have seen today?
Where is my favorite love?
My lasting bliss
It seems an eternity since it has entered me.
Frozen in time away from my grasp

Steeling breathes each moment
Borrowing time to keep it going
How is it that death escapes me?
I have done more than enough to fall into the grave.
Where is It that this forestallment is coming from

Divinest of the most Divine
The Lord has intervened to keep me going.
For the longest time, I have known not why or quite exactly how
Why others who are noble pass on by I am still here

Why is it that we pretend that we are not worthy?
Or that we tell others just the same
Instead of spreading the greatness of the Glory of Heaven
We fall trapped to the Devil's snare.

Our Savior died, so let us not hide our foolish act.
Revel in the truth of the power of God instead
So that even though we are not at first ready for the calling.
Later we will be made to make a stand.
One that will last not a minute or an hour
But for all eternity into a Kingdom that is boundless and beyond measure.

Fantasy

Cooling light and lasting bliss
Waiting For my dearest miss
Beautiful and without transgress
Eyes without lust, guilt, or greed
Body as subtle as full lit moon stars shining all about
Without it, there is nothing but the dark.
All I want is for the truth to come.
To see where we stand and who you think I am
Brightening of hoping for a tremendous, beautiful love
Happiness a long felt never thought fleeting but being beat down.
Giving it all for just one try
Bright and morning waiting for you in the sun
Where the sunny morning light makes your skin glisten
A radiant beauty with all my adoration
Cannot wait to meet you and all your wondrous splendor
Then I can be more beautiful too.
When the sun and the moon meet
I hope your happy your all days.
In all things, love

Enmity

If I could see you now, I would tell you.
Of how I love you and how much I need you
If I knew who you were, we could do things together.
By myself, I am not but empty.
Without another to feel
What is worth feeling
Empty not full
Half laid to rest and adequately rested to breathe.
It is enmity to love the vice of selfishness.
I sought just a moment to be in another world.
One where I could be me, and you could love me for who I truly am
I could drop my fey act and be the one for you.
In the arms of your beauty, I would know just who you are
You are real to me

Holding on To Life

My heart is barely beating.
I have only a moment left to live.
Without love, where will I end up
Without the light, how can I fend off the darkness when I close my eyes?
I remember when I thought I was healthy.
My weakness was something I did not confront
Without true peace of mind and authentic self, I wandered about
It was a cold, cruel world where things did not seem right.
I never felt like I could do right, and I could not feel love
I looked for empty vice and filled my shallow soul.
The confusion of my mind deluded by devilish whimsy.
I fell prey to many a trap and lured to many a pitfall.
Everything was wrong until I opened it.
The word of God blessed me in my troubled times.
I would like to say it happened in a day, but it has taken several more.
I did not know made ignorant by illness.
I was hurting deeper than you could know.
To a sickbed, I did go for such a time to heal my mind.
But broken was still my mind and my soul.
It took great prayer and love, but progress finally came.
God's healing had arrived.
My troubled heart picked up its rhythm.
My soul has begun to heal.
He sent doctors, pastors, friends, family, and most importantly, he sent
the Holy Spirit.
Though I am far from perfect now, I know
How to feel love when it is there and how to communicate love in kind
I am holding on to a life where before I only sought the end.
I did not know how to act.
But now, I am learning how to be a good soldier for the Lord.
I sing in honor and praise and worship in his house.
Where we break bread and rejoice his mighty name

He gives us everything to live for
What is good and what is right
No longer do I always feel so confused.
My mind has grown, and the Lord has taught me many lessons.
The Prince of Peace has given me a new heart.
A gift to show his great compassionate love
Replacing brokenness for fortitude and an ever vigilante protection
I remember the sickbed because it is still not far away.
I have been there more than once
In each time, there was always the word of God
It helped me through to see the truth separate from the insanity.
I am holding on to life because I believe in him, and he makes
it everlasting.
We all can say we are holding on to life so that together we will
stand in Glory.

Embrace You

I am frozen a part without pleading.
Lost without all I am needing.
Cold and frozen without an end
Shivering and crying, a life lost in shape
Fill me and love me
Please hope with all you can
Your embrace will warm my heart forever.
Bring me up and spark my existence.
Lift me and fill me with passion, serenity, and peace of mind
Fever and cold light without order, everlasting love, and grace
Praise the Lord for you as a gift.
I will love you forever should you enjoy me and you with life everlasting.
Blessed by God with pure grace
Flight of a feather or feast of a fancy taste
Breadth of the wind forth with to hasten half fully prepared and under-
girded to demolish my guard
My creed is to protect you, never slander, nor boast against you.
To hold together nor delay love so draw not away.
Lest I go in honor of God without you
I am not intact, never weary nor half weeping.
Fully aware of all that I am seeking, blessed be God's name
For without you, I am not keeping love everlasting or joy divine
I will protect you and serve you.

PART II

SECTION I

Love So Wonderful and Undeniable

Looking for a woman's love most beautiful is the most fulfilling gift from the great God of Heaven. To cleave together to one flesh someday is a prospect that entices us as young as you can dream of it. There are many beautiful women that God has created. Finding one for me has been what I have wanted most in my entire life. So many enticing beauties there are, and yet for a while, we are all alone. All we want is love wonderful, and to be denied love is to be rejected, the greatest gift to man from God. A helpmate and a beautiful soul. You are to treat her beauty higher than you would yourself. For Christ's Love for the Church should always be steeped in your actions. All I want is love, so wonderful and undeniable.

Again, To Love

Ode to love greatness, tears, fondness, and delight
Serenity bond and truth, I love you, my lady, you are good to me,
sweet and charming
Vexed me not apposed gentle and merciful
Could make even a man blush as I used to as a child
Having a hard time living in the moment
No longer will I cry without love
Rain like it rains and drown out my sorrow.
Thank you for your tears; they warmed my heart
Dearest lady, you are beautiful as could be

Big River Flowing Deep

Flow deep big river running wide wading slowing water path
Cool breeze and a fogging wind running around a while
Creeping down a road, I see you tired, bedraggled.
I would pick you up and hold you if you would let me.
I am not weak any longer; I am more energetic, growing day by day.

Night by night, I am not lying.
I am dying to see you when I am weary.

Hold each other in our arms, be a touch ahead.
From here to their nobody looking our way, just cutting in
I am traveling on, want you to sing along.
Cutting through the clear
Hope you miss me
Cause tomorrow I will be gone just traveling on.
Do not want to lose; I just want to kiss you and hold right on.

Do You Hear Me Now?

I am alive and well, running and soaring.
Picking up speed no longer distant or dissonant
What a grand journey from here to there, never-ceasing, never done,
always competing.
Sticking up to all the discontent and destructive malice
Soft felt hands of creation forestalling the turbulence.
Continuing never defeated
Do you hear me now when I say I am kind and well?
Or when I bespoke to you all my confidence and concise repartee.
Should I hide from you again or just let it be and then shout
What I feel and where I am
In this land of difference
Making all things new
I am in a fresh breath, a new creature through and through
A beast with wings instead of fangs upon the morning sky
Looking for a place to land and nestle for a night
Stopping in the starlit sky
Finding a new home

Never Stay Gone Long

I will come back to you never to leave without saying goodbye.
Running through the wind, never running away without going too far.
Wading through the wind like a wisp and with gentlemen's tact
To hear your voice makes me enthralled.
Like a stud running through the valley searching for a mate

Song for Her

Sweet as could be, you are
Lovely as could be
Compassion, peace, and mercy
In your heart, I will survive.
Taking sweet surrender
In your arms, I will survive.
You are very lovely and tender in your touch.

So, embrace me and hold me.
Do not send me away
I will run to your arms and dance the night away.

She is altogether sacred to me.
My precious jewel survives.
I love your deep surrender.
I want you by my side.

Morning

Today the sky tomorrow a morning beauty.
As the sun rises and you wake, most precious and quixotic.
Taking me unaware and surprising me with rapturous delight
The sunlight is outstripped by the radiance glowing from your face.
I see you as the most significant every time I see you smile.
Brightening up my day, making my heart skip and jump inside
Eve of my dawn, the most magnificent sound I have heard.
Tethered to my ear your gleeful laughter and a meaningful joy to me
I know that I appreciate all you do for me.
The gaze in your eyes touching and entrancing.
I love the way you move and sway moving all-day.
When night sets in, and we part our ways
I will think of you and done today, waiting for another morning.
The next morning, I see your grace.

Fruit of a Blossom

Taste of refinement encapsulating to my eyes
Tears shed watering the flowers and the groves where the roses grow.
Pluck my bleeding heart and enrapture my soul
Saved for the season waiting for both me and for you
Caught between a lamp and a stand grand today tomorrow another
Love in your eyes and the tears that you cried
Stunning a beauty never seen before without eclipse
Lovely tasteful, and with a lavender kiss

Forever and a Dream

Second to none and forever and for more
Taste of Burgundy
Stars of Sapphire, Onyx, and Beryl
Shouts of joy and rapturous rain
Tantamount to the feeling of a hot drizzle of a morning dew
Manna of my life taste of forever
Lovely as precious hummingbird fluttering in my ear
Twitch of fancy bird of flight nestling in a country willow
Will I rest waiting for my love where o' where you have gone?

Blanket in the Snow

Unwrapped on the doorstep of a frame half stepped backward three
folded thrice, where does it fit?
Backward in time, if I could go there, I would not
The future is in your eyes precious as could be
Lay back down and see no longer
Rising tide and flooding wheel face to face
Side to side hips and glide carry you away.
Float to the rooftops and with a blanket of snow
The warmth from each other glistening and sending each other away
Depths of the deep and the heat of the passion
Do not lurk nor watch for the blinding of the sun.
The melting of the snow in the wind of winters chill

Tree of the Wild

Exotica, Trance, Epic, Prose
Rain, Lightning, Wind, Nature

Tree of the Wild
Tree of the Second Coming
Light of the Earth
Salt of the Sand

Rain, Lightning, Wind, Nature
Merriment, Passion, Style, Affection

Light of the Earth
Salt of the Sand
Beauty of the Insurrection
Sweetness of the Sound

Flee to the Harbor

Running to shore from an ill-begotten plane.
Never hearing your voice deaf from death's ring not finding a place
for safe harbor.
Rushing to an everyday long-forgotten faith untethered
Fighting for my life turn of the wheel
God-given strength growing and fading.
And I saw the Light come crashing in.

Rain in the Wind

Running deep and crashing, washing ashore, and waking up in a blur.
Finding my knees running in and dancing sleeping in
Off like a blur and sleeping, taking a second step.
Rain cascading and flying through the deep to a second breathe.
Rain in the air slowing still and washing ashore
Quick breeze and trapping wind
Thanking the Lord for all the blessings of the blessed times
Sweet as they are, holding on for longer and longer
Rain in the wind
Water under the wing
Floating still shining proud
Trending weary running true
Flying through the wind, I wake up in the sand.
Always looking for my growth, waiting to breakthrough.
Refined and not debased
Let it not end until I find it again.

Looking for a Miracle

Coming back from running away, falling short, and going astray
Looking for a miracle to stop my false pride
Taking to old habits
Trying to better myself and keep it from consuming me.
Looking for an in not a cop-out from my mind
Blocking myself from freedom, looking away from peace of mind
Forgetting what I have said, looking to be more lovely
Cannot stop being lost in my past
Fleeing though it is
The bad times are emptying from my mind.
Like a grove, my confidence is growing.
Bettering myself day by day
Learning to master my mind and delineate my soul
So, wake up; it is time to go free.
Still looking for my miracle.
That is what it is to me.

Baptized in Your Eyes

Thank you so much for your eyes, words, and your tears
I was dying and fearing for it all.
Do not know where to turn and to do what at all.
I was tired of myself, my past fear, and my unaccomplished hopes.

I am living, breathing, and dying for a new dream.
Of satisfying my soul and living a righteous life
Upright true and free, I am living for a new dedication.
No self-destruction or false tribulation
I am waking up more beautiful.
Less hurt or pained, only tired of falling so far
So, wake up and dream with me.
I am looking at the stars.
With a little bit of apprehension
Just waiting in the moment and loving all the while
I just want to be baptized in your eyes.

Just Wondering Why

Leaning into a new wonderment, taking my last step
Sickness left; I am undoubtedly blessed.
Not skipping a beat, hoping for a way to take the lead.
I am on my feet, still wondering why
I could not stop and try.
Could not wonder why I am doing what I did
I ran away, looked too far away.
And now I am waking up to a new time.
Heading not disobeying
Thank you for what you are doing
Thank you, o,' Lord for the touch
The sympathy and the gain
Increase it further and eschew a new conscience into me
Run me around, work me up higher into the ladder of your worship
Let me lead and honor you.

Do Not Harken

Do not call unless bidden; do not unlock unless given the key.
Sticks or resin rhyme or song
Beckon do not call
Bring it nearer into the night and run it far away.
Close the door and open the key
Three knocks down four clicks west
Seventh nine of three eights
Quarter twist and five backs eight
Do not touch the star-struck straight.
Lest it fall and you become broken far
Please pick it up and draw a sentimental token; take it back.
Run around and rise in the west
Run into a bind, never check a lead

Giving Without End

Turn forward, not back, and never rest without giving.
Helping each other conquering when weary
In each other arms and outside my grasp
Looking forever for what I have not got until the end at last
Holding and moving, not running astray
Moving abounding in fire
Twisting and turning, not looking with ire
Run to the cold metal heat dimming the steel
Running a beauty half churned fully engraved.
Forged in the ice and the fire of heat
Melting in rain
Cooling in fire
Heat of passion
Fire of ice

Quiver Softly

Came down for a break in the middle of the sun shining
Running out bleak and still taking to snow.
Sheets of ice slick and treaded
Bleak once it was now melting in me
Raising through the sound of a dove.
A soft quiver from the breeze as it goes by
Walking through the air sleeping in the trees
Taking a nap fell by the swell, a gust in the wind.
Quiver softly sweet dove
Wake in the morning, sleep through the evening.
Painstaking rest
Worthwhile tract
Looking up
Gazing back and going to sleep

Great Submission

Growing heart submissive love
Great leaps untethered bounds.
Sweltering in the heat of the fire
Gathering in the deep of the woods
Generous to one another
From one end up over the other
One day to the next
From another day to the first
Beginning and the end
Freest mind
Abounding love with abundant joy
Someday it will be great to be with you.
Holding on to my one dream to live and to love
Never to die nor fade away.
Picking it up and redeeming it in my way

SECTION II

Floating

In the heavens far and wide stunning and wonderous
Floating through space, the heavenly bodies apace.
Wondering what is all out there and where I will end up
In another time, place, and galaxy
What planet will I end up on, and what will it be like
Will I be alone on a barren rock?
Or at peace on a beach in a paradise
Will, there be others, and what will they be like
Are they created like you and me?
I hope there as engaging and worthwhile as your company.
Apace a green sea of tranquility, a gorgeous orchard filled with fruit.
On this planet, unencumbered by what I left behind
Deaf to past transgressions, open and free to live in a honied land
Sweet as the Garden of Eden and as promising in turn
Glad to be here planet new and exciting
Far away from the troubles of Earth.

One day only

If only one day my dreams would rest
Hide dry up and loosen
Bend back and sleep
Grow weary, die and be reborn
Resurrected to Glory
Freedom of the best sort
Hiding in the clouds taking a nap
Pacing around thinking by the Garden with gain
Mercy is the forest of hackberry with meager tasteful fruit.
Bearing great abundance and trying to tamp down the hunger for more
Blessings be upon your night delight in the rest.
Great long mornings to follow in the breath of your spirit
No shadows cast apart weary nor ransomed.
Hottest swelter smitten by the heat
Cooled by the gaze of the heavens
Magnified by a starlit complexion
Growing in magnification
Intensity of your blessed love
Bring me all my feelings of compassion.
Turn me into a real maker and molder.
Star breaker shadow bent
Line up from the backward cast and entrance
Vibrations of passion
Clairvoyance of the mind
Indignation of the spirit
Kindness of your highest intent
Blessing be upon you as you rest into the night.

Entangled

Conjoining together into a whimsical fashion
Not for a short time or rope but an extended enthralling gathering
Brought together unbeknownst to my mind
Not having sought you but abutting, nonetheless.
Anything but trite a cacophony of your love
Wrapped together and never shunned by my curious mind
Never dreamt of an entanglement so beautiful my brain could not fathom
Someone so dignified that could not see
What it is I see in you though you do not know.
How you brighten my day even for a moment
A peaceful moment where I remember to smile
A smile that, for me that is hard to come by
Robbed of my happiness and replaced with shattered reverence
Oh, how you do not know what you do to me

Shadow Guard

Call upon the sword
Shield and bracers are broken.
One last night taken aback, unabashed unashamed.
Cloak and dagger enemy of my strongest vice
Emptying my blood flowing strength of my God
Bloodshed on the rocks at the hill
Fighting, I am called back to the line.
Last to hold my enemy filled with deceit
Bloodied screams and merciless swings
Death to the days and fall swells from tomorrow.
Destruction of today corruption breading tomorrow
Final call for the brave
Meet at the hill tonight; we die forever; we live.
Cutting through the pain and the dissatisfaction of conflict
Bringing the fight back and cutting through the death and decay
Delving through the last of insanity pulling through to the Shadow Guard
We will keep you from going down and being dealt a swift
We are the Shadow Guard

Drawing Conclusions

The end, beginning, the in-between.
It is tough to tell where we stand back against a wall.
Other times we are busting through sledgehammer and ax to grind.
From the time we are born until the time we die.
We slam through the hardest rock.
We cut through the most robust trees.
Carry the biggest loads
Fight the most challenging fights.

No drawing conclusions on us
You are not the Judge.
Nor the Jury
We are the in-between.

The Jump

Sauntering out of town, not looking for a ride or way home
Taken aback by my last vice looking for death to run
Walking and waiting
Raining and gusting
Out of body flying in the air
Dreading moving to this place, never contemplating
Hurt that builds and never ceases
Falling and falling, I never rise.
Why can I not find what I am looking for
Am I still alive?
Because it did not feel like it
Not until now
Does it hurt?
You could not imagine
Where are you?
Still jumping
Until now
For I have awoken in grace
The Lord has eased my mind.
Saved my troubled soul
Took me from the air
I fall short, but he aims true.
He disconnected my sorrows.
And bled my farewells.
Woke up my eyelids and depressed my false conjecture
So now, as I rise, I do so in peace.
Until forever in Glory.

SECTION III

Spirit Flow

Moving free set thereof by a mindful Lord
Bonding together in his presence, sacrificing bloodshed
I wake up looking for a new way to partake.
A new communion to indulge in
No more running dry and lost in the desert.
Hung out and strung out on an itch, a passion for a new kind of love
One without lust, anger, and vengeance
One lacking false pride and reckless drudgery
Fruits unabating
Given a gift of togetherness
No longer separated, finding each other.
Flow spirit flow
Lock us together, bring us near
Let us love and show compassion.
Never wavering and losing our sights on each other.
Let you and I love each other as if we were never apart.
Together in strength
Flow spirit flow
Make me a lover
Stop me from being a woeful sinner.
Bring me a light and torch.
A sword, shield, arrow, and quiver
Bow to strike the target set on the heart
So, look out for loves arrow and let your mind rest.
Altogether in love as the spirit flows.

Beautiful Surrender

You look so vibrant and altogether beautiful to me.
So, surrender with me, and let us love together.
A God whose passion, mercy, kindness, and truth are unsurpassed
The glory made you of God.
He who shines through every time you smile, and
Whenever your grace adorned with all the festive vibrance of your heart
You speak truth in kindness, and when you say I love you
God is in your ears, and he has them all the while
So just say that you love me and give me your hand.
We can walk together forever in the holiest of lands.
The real promise of eternal Glory and bliss
Through sacrifice, we do enter.
His hope is forever, so let us make it you and me.
Because I will love you persistently
Your beautiful surrender
Keeps me going every single day

Flower

A great flowering lady
One day an Eve tomorrow an evening beauty
Together an Adam
Hope for a day when I see you tomorrow
Love from now till forever, I invite you to the deep blue sky
In the depths of the rain, I will give you a kiss.
Rub your back and give you all the love that I can
From the end of today to the light of tomorrow
A light breeze and a faint shadow
Love, you gave me feeling so great.
It runs deep in my veins.
Your passion makes me weak on bended knee.
Your hair so sweet
Hands light and touch so soft it makes me feel relieved
Beautiful so beautiful
I want to dance with you on a wisp in the wind.
Love you forever with all that I have
Kindness for my best friend sweetness and a kiss with all my heart
Tender hugs and sweet eyes
Prettiness served well in your embrace.
Women of a splendid bosom filled with bliss
Touch of a lady who knows what it takes
To keep me intact

Where I Stand

I am coming down from my self-idealized paradise.
Sometimes it is tough to see where I stand.
Am I here where the cactus is my only shade parched and dry?
Or over there in the magnificent oasis where water springs are glorious
Or yet stuck down in a pit where pride ensnares an unenlightened soul.
Today I am crawling out of my hole and freeing myself.
Though I have been parched, dry, and dying
Now I am renewed by the oasis.
The spring of unfathomable plenty
The fruits of plenty with great taste and luxury
Still, it compared nothing to the God that is
For this is man's vice that we should wander
Sometimes with no drink and others with plenty
The pits and the overcoming digging in and climbing out
Until one day, you realized there is greater glory in God.
Then there is always the living water, the bread of life, the magnificent
gardens of God.
This Garden is where I stand.

Tears at Night

Up all day, burdened at night.
Never a day where I can seem to stem the flow
Death from my eyes and the burning desire
It is the passion and the pain that is retaking me.
Waking me up every day, I am calling out for my life anew.
Turning and churning, burning, and burning, waiting for the
blood to pass by
Cannot stop these tears at night
It is a desire I seek a playful last memory.
A dance without death but forever on
Walking on lightning and hammering rain
Clouds unending and closing springs end twain.
I just want to stop these tears at night.
But I know I cannot because I care too much.
Without a care, I would be nowhere and with no one.
Just wake me up in the morning.
After I have cried myself to sleep at night

Heavens Embrace

I lift you high to the greatest of embraces.
Your greatest love
Your sweet embrace
You are beautiful
You are lovely, love.

You tempt me to wonder what it would be like if there were no others.
Only you and me together in the air
Its Heavens embrace dancing in the stars.
The sunlight on the beach or the frost on the valley
My difference you are the same
Dew in the valley
And light in the plains.
To the highest of mountains
To the deepest of caves
No longer lonely
Just looking for another verb for love everlasting
Because Heaven would not be anything without you in my arms

Your greatest love
Your sweet embrace
You are beautiful
You are lovely, love.

SECTION IV

Words from Another

Sometimes we see short-sighted what we should in full.
A figure unabashed created with divine inspiration
A heart filled with not half-truths but filled with forgiving compassion
We see each other, not through the lenses of God.
But through the tired meager eyes of years of pain.
Past the pain is the beauty inside
Beauty that I see every time I see you
Whenever I cry, I wish you were there to dry the tears.
Where is my endless love?
Where could she be this beauty of mine?
I have been looking for some time.
I am wild and parched.
Stripped bare and on my last end
Looking for wonderful love
Her grace that makes the heavens shake
The sound of her radiance that makes me bow my head at night
I have half a heart left, the other half wounded.
Sliced by pains and pitiful trials
Not hearing the voices of iniquity, I listen to your call.
Come to me and call upon my heart.
Together we can be whole.
Those words from another are what it is all for

Dead and Bleeding Living and Dying for You

Blood dripping from my brow getting beat
Waking up and dying from my head to my feat
Looking for the end until I see you
Now I want to be living and dying for you.
So, I tamp the blood and spit out the rest because I am a fighter for you.
No rest in the heat of battle, not the last one to end them all either
Rising from the pool of my death, I come.
My previous still wound covered by the presence of your thought.
This wound is not healing; without your love, this heart is still bleeding.
Dying and bleeding, I pull out the last arrow make my final charge.
Because for you, I fight beyond death into the spirit
Conquering the grave rebirthed and re-raised, I fight for your time.
Looking to be your last thought on this Earth until reunited in Heaven
Then when this war is over, we will love like no other.
Brought together and healed of our scars
After the God and I servant, bring the Devil to his improvisation and send
him far from you.
We will forever dance and embrace sweet and tender.
With all the joy, we will sing and praise
Together forever in his Grace
Lovers to the end

Awkward Journey

Stumbling, I come in from far away, dropping in and letting loose.
Picking up where I left off without the hanging noose
Looking for the pain to set in again
As I take this awkward journey, I am alone.
A stumbling bum with nowhere to call home
Nobody to call me a hero nor to pacify my woeful demeanor.
I am a lonely man who does better on his own
Not looking for a way out, just an outlaw.
On the run again, a one-person militia.
Takes a team to take out this fury
What one woman could do with a glance
Pacify this hungry beast and quell the rage within
I am working on a new wonder.
Falling into this new world, I am in
It is time to end this awkward journey.

Beauty from West

Love from the west on to the scent of the most refined oils
Lavender and black licorice spice added to the mix
The scent of a thousand loves
Set on heavenly intent
A beautiful morning running and skipping a beat.
From the arbiter of the exotic
The love of my life
An existential heart beating with mine
Running around with purpose to support a lovely heart, a twitter opposed.
Shattered and lovely recomposed.
An altruistic countenance a splendor exquisite
A crash at the pad a flower of the best scent
My spirit awakened the soul of a babe.
A woman so beautiful a taste worth the most excellent
cinnamon and spice
So magnificent and beautiful finer than Kashmir wool and silk
Hair worth its weight in silk
One of real intent purest love

PART III

SECTION I

To All and Love

It is a time to continue fighting for what we enjoy the trueness of God's bliss from where we are from and where we will go; love is always in store. From family or another looking for what is in store. We are beginning in life, never-ending in death, for we will be reborn again. It is my most resounding of hopes that we will all meet again together in Glory. Heaven will be sweet, boisterous, and exquisite. A marriage between God and the Church. To the Son, the Father, and the Holy Spirit, we all pray our prayers most anxious.

Looking forward to the future where all will be at peace, the enemy laid bare. Again, I hope to be in Christ with thee. Blessing of the purest Spirit.

Let it run

You cannot cage an animal lest you tame its soul.
This monster has no time for the tame or of the like
Running from field-to-field maiming where it can
Tackling false ambitions and swooning over lust-filled lies
A boon to my pet, he roars and conquers in my name.
Killing the fell beasts and demons to keep me sane
Conquering the deep divide, this sinner gone to hide.
So, do not come looking for the cave I am in.
I am hiding underground deep where the den of the monster is
Do not poke the beast lest you look to cut off his fell head.
Do not unleash the bird of prey if prey is all you are
A small meal only to satisfy for a day.
One single day cannot last forever.
And that is what I am looking for is a home to call my own
Far away from my untamed beast

Running Wild

Encumbered no longer running free, born wild
Traversing the trees and rolling in the dirt
Reckless and dangerous riding the air through the forest
Plucking the wild berries of bliss, just one wrong one spells the end.
Sometimes an embrace thought longingly to end just to begin.
Tired of a lonely waggling life
Fleeting and unembroidered uncouth and unadorned
A temple without a tapestry
One fell swoop and a fatal noise, one last cry never to hear again.
Curling and twirling screaming and dying.
Why do I still live this life?
Is it only to say that I am not weak?
It makes me feel no stronger.
A lion without a pride, stabbed and tortured.
A pet of the enemy was captured and kicked in the dirt.
Would somebody let me loose and bust these chains to free
my mortal soul?
So, I can wake and slumber no longer.
Tame this tortured beast

Ripple Effect

Drowning in the water and barely floating
After surfacing many miles from shore
In a different land, an island unfamiliar.
No rescue nor company my usual tasteless treats
Creating my entertainment in my addled mind
Creeping and sinking tossing stones while passing time
Waiting on this deserted shore for someone to join
To make this land more peaceful.
To join me in song
To live and laugh like no one else.
Being the last two in the world is something we would feel.
As we dance and run and feed on wild fruit
With few animals to keep company lest we tempt the dangerous wild
Lost and tethered together stuck two persons were
Dreamt of a day when we could wash ashore across the way
Grow apart and forget our time but change others with our last days
We would have had each other if only we had stayed.
But insanity was setting in, and we ran away.
To the peace of pure society
Where we never were alone
But now, without you, I will forever know the feeling.

Bathed in Blood

Weapons like nail-scarred hands
Looking through the eyes of another
Not seeing as I should
Hoping to awaken from this sin
Caught up in it and taken away from myself and who I am
Bathe me in the blood of the Lamb
Wash me anew and let it stand as my cleansing feat
Tear apart the false ideology that is cursing my life
Never good enough, consistently weak, and afraid
Cannot stand without a crutch and cannot sleep without
the terror of mind
Never forget what has been and how it strangled my thoughts.
Perverted my brain and stabbed my soul with a sharpened knife
So, I clean my soul with the blood of the Lamb that I can renew who I am
Hating that I could be so much more by now if it were not for the lies
Looking for blessings from above
I am someone to love, but all I could feel was distorted hate.
Wondering why it could happen as only a child
But why God do not you save me and stop this mindless gathering.
Now I take my weapons like nail-scarred hands and put them to use
Picking up the pieces of my shattered mind
Pulling together my soul and patching it with cloth
Soaking up the blood from my bleeding heart, sewing up the wound
Waking up anew
I am still alive and breathing.
Not sinking and feeling down
But picking up and fighting for God and myself.
That I can be a warrior for you and me

Breaking Free

Waking up ensnared by my demons
Painstaking life-taking, and full of woe
Captured and imprisoned
My last venture took me to this place.
But now that I have had time to contemplate.
I am breaking free, cutting the ties that bind.
Asserting my strongest will and watching that wily old serpent flee
A new man with convictions bold and true
Looking for others to tell this story to
Of how I broke free from the devil's cunning snare
Fleeing from the devourer of souls into the open arms
Of Jesus Christ, the one authentic way
The one who will never do me harm

Racing By

My last broken leg snapping into place, waking up for the moun-
tain that I face
Climbing and climbing weak-kneed and shattered ankles
Straining with every step
I see you racing by running where I am struggling.
So why don't you lend me some of your strength?
You have more than enough.
So, I can also run, dear brother.
Then we can both make it to the top.
Where the kingdom lies, and forever, we will be best friends.
Let us leave our mark on this world and not just keep racing by
Looking for others without our strength and legs to stand
So, they can join us, and together, we will land.
All together in the most fabulous paradise
Where we can join Jesus after we make this final run

Tasteful and Elegant

Honestly, I would love to live in a different time and place.
A time more tasteful and more elegant
Where we would not hide inside our passion and our love
Where we would do things in this present moment and not hide
from each other
Where we would live with wit and laugh merry in one another's arms
This bliss and compassion are what I deeply miss.
To be a loved one after another, I cannot sink without feeling
this life's bliss.
I would now like to tell you how I think I am falling and need
you to pick me up.
I am a failure, and I am losing without a wit to meet an end.
Not buying into my promise to live most elegant and full of grace.
Without a beauty, my grace dissipates falls with me out of my grasp.
I am alone wanderer a man whose cold and given unto dereliction.
Not doing my duty, failing the Lord, and not committing
to my conviction.
A taste of love is all I ask, one last sip from an empty cup.
Or you could come and just fill it up.
Then we could live in peace and mercy and cure my feeble twitch.

Roaring Thunder

They call me thunder because I come with the loudest storm.
Wind gusts and lightning thrust blowing through the land
Destruction comes, but when I am fleeting and calm, you know it is un-
doubtedly at the end.
Never question whether to be cautious around the beaten rain.
It is plentiful and thick this time and will drown you and me together.
We cannot escape the grasp of nature.
Should not try
What we must do is to comply and ride out the storm.
Together you and I
The lightning and the thunder
Natures natural best of friends
We break the backs of any pine and spark desire in any eye.
Followed by the beautiful rainbow shining in my mind
Oh, glorious rain brought from the heavens.
So, you and I, the lightning, and the thunder.
Can travel together again

Laughter in the Rain

Waking up in the spring looking at the finest of the greenery
Shadowing each other meeting together from time to time
When the rain comes and left without a shelter
Together we laugh in the rain.
Happy with nothing else, not another person in our sights
We walk and run
Dance and light up a new romance
Your sweet churning and body turning.
It is your laughter in the rain.
All that is keeping me sane to end the day
For without this bliss and a final kiss
This dance, this trance
This happenstance
Together in the rain

Tortured Soul

Aggregated into small cavern-like cattle
I am burnt up and strung out and taken out into the deepest depths.
This soul has been misused and abused.
Tortured and berated
Choked off and misappropriated
Looking for a way to look up and get out of the cavern
A journey through death and the deepest of restless nights
I have kept alive, barely stringing along through the depths of
an addled mind.
Do not fly away; do not idle off and let the creature out of the
boisterous deep.
Hide no longer from the fear, for I am slaying the monster to escape with
the last of the tattered soul
Cut off the head and deliver myself from this frightful foe.

Windmill Crossings

A pure breeze and a twisted mane turning 'round for me again
Shadows light and dawns sweet darkness.
A light bright and starry, darkness weak and bleary
Walking through the daisies looking for my twain, my arch,
and morning grain
A feast of fancy, a high fill, a morning picnic without a basket
Sweet blanket and sweet wine
Cherry cider and apples dining on the fruits so fine
Lovely my most considerable fortune pricks my side and pinches
me out of dream.
For dream, this must be to be beautiful and to glisten with all of thee.
Thine beauty is the apple and the cherry cider, a taste of your sweet kiss.
All the while sipping the wine of all your greatest delight

Delight of My Heart

High and weary meek and kind
Humble and fabulous, this gorgeous woman so fine
Brisk and merciful wisp
A fantastic head of hair and smile, thus invoking so stirring of the heart.
Why don't you find time to string me along a path?
That way, we can walk together, and I can know your hidden soul.
What makes you hide, cry, laugh, fear
Do you seek love like me?
Or a fleeting last goodbye
I hide from love because I am a little shy.
Do not take risks on this because I am not used to knowing what it is like
I never thought myself a handsome man, dashing, daring, nor bold.
Merely a shadow of what I should be a king without a hold.
Mighty benevolence of truce and faith
I seek greatness and love forever.
With the kindness of your grace

When Will I Die?

Where will I be in the end o' where
Will I be in a mistress's arms?
Or by myself, as I often am lonely and fleeting by myself.
By thy lonesome query, I shall surely die.
I do not do as I should, not strong enough to make a life for myself
filled with another.
When will I die?
What day will it happen?
To never feel that feeling deep inside the one that only could be brought
by another's glance.
By myself to the depths of my dreadful soul
That is my greatest fear.
To never taste what others know.
To never feast on the antiquities of the purest of desires.
To never be together parting only jaunt away yet miles in between
Further and farther
Never but fleeting seeing you today.

Crushing Spirit

Spirit exposed and trials of woe.
Never did I ever know what would happen when this journey started
Would I appear when I could or go to the land of the dually departed
Shall I go now to the darkest corner of my soul?
Shattered and broken of spirit fold
Rooted and tainting my heart to the very core
This abyss is not of bliss; this crushing spirit that is taking hold.
Running afoul of my happiness and ruining my desire.
To carry on in my humble stead a genuine aspiration for a bed to lie in
Waking up to a still-beating heart looking for a cure
To this broken heart
Looking to be on the mend from this blow
A crushing spirit has indeed dealt.

You Are Not Alone

When you think that all is lost, and you feel unwelcome in yourself
I want you to know that you are not alone.
Exploring outside of your comfort and placed in dissatisfaction
I would bring you back out of it if I could, but I do not know
where to start.
Blessed hope and bright, filled thoughts the beauty arraigned within
Your brightness and your glow will instill within you every day.
Have a peace where you are now
Even better for tomorrow
I have been there in pain. I felt it all my life.
I would hate for any to know where I have been before
It is a taciturn tale of woe.
They cast it all on me, and it was never known.
But I want you to know that you are not alone.

Deaths Final Blow

An awkward end to a heartfelt, passionate entanglement
Glory gone and distance made more accurate from thy embrace.
Verily as I sleep this night, I am dealing the final blow.
Out of mind and sanity cast afar
Boldly as I die, it is my last cry to look for you hereafter.
Would you ever forgive me?
I never did what I promised or what I dreamed I would do.
Not near a man, the man I should have been
As I lay in deaths embrace
Heart ceasing, my last tremble trickles down a last choking breathe.
Save me o' Lord for my life I want renewed.
Should he renew as we can trust him to
I will find you and tell you why
I cannot breathe without your eyes.
How long I have admired from afar
Stunning and a flare like a wildfire tangle within you
When will I see you again after this bleary end?
For you see, our spirits live forever on, and yours is undoubtedly true.
More confident than I ever am
More courageous than I ever was
I see you in the kingdom, not just a passerby.
Someday we will meet in Glory.
For me, it is a wonder why
You could ever stand to be by this man.
Knowing where I have been and who I was
Taken from a horror to look for a better future
No season on the Earth is more blessed.
Nor tree anticipated with fresh enduring scent
Harmony and accord never fashion without a sense.
My bleary, ripping pain will not last long.
I want to be forever in your arms.
Where death will succumb the final blow

Through the Fires of Hell

I have been through crooked flames.
Cried out, crawled around, and tried to hide all my shame
Broken bones and shattered reverie
Turning around in the disastrous pit of the lies
I burn again, but I am not giving in.
Never falling straight or headfirst in the lake.
I will arise when it is time to sink or swim.
Distant memories fading away, starting to soothe my burns
I walked through the fires of hell and survived.
All because he is on my side
The blessed one of Bethlehem
Brightest one of Heaven brings me up with you.
Take away my strife and make me whole again.
Bury this hole and tamp this fire
So, I can breathe again without all this smoke.

Born of Fire

By flame of boldness upright and true brazen and crass
Unduly ended to have risen from the fire.
Mortar bearing could not blast it.
Hell could not defeat it.
No army on Earth can contain it nor stop its growing intensity.
My spirit has emboldened, and I shall never die.
For Christ has died that we shall live forever by his side.
With flaming sword and compassionate tongue
The world is in need.
Driving back Hell's gates and delivering us from evil
Descending from the heavens bringing the fire to deny it passage
Never cross us foes, for we surely do not die.
For an army of angels and the Lord, God is on our side.
You can do all in earthly means to try to extinguish the flame.
But it will be reborn again.
Birthed rebirthed, and born
Turned around again
Brought to life to enter peace
By defending true and virtues, mighty
With our God and with each other
We make ourselves insurmountable.
A fool to be an enemy.
For the power of our savior will defeat wrath, envy, and all the
greed in the world.
The serpent's sure defeat

Burning Stars

Fanning the flame
Cooling it down to tame the spirit
The beast was slain and rest to begin.
We shine like stars heating the world and providing essential life.
Taking comfort in a new Heaven and new Earth
To what will be and what shall we do when shall it and how wonderful.
Reign of righteousness the shining of the brightest burning star
Great Lord and rock of all creation
Reuniting us all together triumphant and true
Make me a mighty man in your kingdom do with me all you will
I would just like to be with all that extraordinary beauty.
For with all that you created
Woman came from man
We never forget where we are from and who created us.
Never do we know who we will love until your light shines upon us
To unite us like you a burning star high and mighty fire of the world.
Sentiment aside, I would be a warrior should they be needed.
Never rest the flaming sword; be a guard and worship the Holy Spirit.
Burning ones welcome me as I come into my place.

SECTION II

Astonish

Bright wonders and enlightenment truths have never been told.
To wake up in the new light is a golden fortune worth more than
a thousand-fold.
Astonished by a more exceptional being and greatness untold
A new person with breathing not choking in a false hold
Painting a picture of prosperity in a land once thought fantasy.
To see a great desire beheld fresh and blessed by the Glory of our God.
King of King's mighty redeemer
Prepare us a place like in the land of Galilee.
A room prepared before the wedding
A wedding feast fit with all lavishness.
To whom will dine and who shall come
To gather in Heaven's trinity.
For up above with wings of a dove
We ascending to blessing, peace, and love
Forever into infinity
Astonished

Besotted

Dearly and truthfully, I share with you nearly.
Of divinity in your spirit
God imparting all the beauty he could to blossom you in a wondrous style.
You never knew what I saw in you or never what I am
More than a brute or a fool among the foolish
Do not question my love, for I am weak and bending.
Not a pretend fancy nor fleeting and frightful.
Maybe once a fool but not forever
Growing and fanning looking and fawning.
Happy as a newborn babe looking for his mother
Gracious love, undying passion, and mercy for my past misdeeds
Forgive me for my profanity.
I was, but a broken man, a shell of the veracity indwelt
My dear, I am besotted with the idea of meeting you.
In a specific time or place
I know that your countenance is as radiant as could be
Effervescent and likened unto a perfect hue
A shade not seen nor ever beheld a freedom in my heart
God has shed his grace on me.
I will know when we meet.

Mothers Arms

The first woman to love us
In the arms of a mother
Birthing us and caring for us while we grow and learn to walk
Great provider and nurturer highest of our regards
Carrying us for all that time protection and the great gift of life
Feeding us and dressing us smiling all the while
My first gift a wondrous life
Parents who taught me Jesus and the love he has in store
That he knows us even before we formed
In our mother's womb
Teaching us a love for women and giving us great insight
To find our own and be a lover and make a woman a mother of her own
So, we can be a father and in goodness rear.
Children of our own

Father

Our fathers teach us sons how to be a man.
How to work and dig the dirt
Try to keep us from the troubles that they know exist.
Teach us how to pray for supper and to build
So, we can prepare a life for ourselves and make our way into the world.
They stick up for us and lead the way back home.
Like a prodigal son when we have indeed failed
Together with our mother, they do not give up on us.
They get us back on track and work with us to instill
What we learned when we were young and how to relearn
The love for others even when we lose all hope
That we can venture out and trust again
But remember where we have been
So, we do not slide and go back.
To be a prodigal again.

Strong Man

Bearing strength to tackle the toughest of tasks lifting all the weight upon
strong shoulders
Load bearing legs moving and moving, keeping on under pressure.
Taking it all in and working to be stronger
Sometimes forgetting when to be weak and soft.
Never ceasing to be a bearer of the burdens.
Breaking not under pressure nor stopping till the end
Toiling onward striking no barter for easy passage
Looking for a night to stop and rest along the way
A break from this monstrosity to coalesce with you someday,
So, I do not have to pretend to be strong for so long, and I
can be who I am
By staying still and looking deeply at you and sharing my soul
A peaceful stay from pretension where I value myself again
For with you, I am not alone, not in part but a whole
Deep tranquility with you
Hoping it lasts
Amen

Moonlit

The darkness of the night sky waiting to prowl deep in the wild
Looking for a den to crawl in, a wolf separated from the pack.
Howl at the moon, looking for others to join
To start a new pack and to gather for the hunt.
Then we can creep about
Looking for new grounds to call our own
Claim the land and take the prey making a kill to keep our fill
The life of a wolf on the move escaping death day by day
and moonlit night
Looking for another alpha a mate to make a pack
This hunger creeping in to take me far away
Where I can find what I seek
A world where I am not the omega
Standing tall and winning the battles.
Picking fights that I will surely win
Running astride and side by side.
Two wolves to start a travel.

Christic in You

I want to see the beauty of the way God created you.
With thought to each detail and ever-loving care
I want to see all of you the idea that God intended.
Glorious how beautiful your indwelling spirit is so fine
To touch it with care, kindness, and concern.
To meet your soul would be an uplifting experience.
One that fills with joy, growth, and purest of delight
To learn and bond together in the holiest of the lights.
Bearing in mind a kindred spirit is tough to find
I hope to find one so lovely.
Then trepidation can dissolve in our presence.
I want to see the Christ in you, the shining of the light.
Shining in like a candle in the dark
Lighting up a sky, lighting in the clouds
The moon overhead with all the stars beaming and bright seen
from so far away
Fawning over you like the most aromatic scent stemming from the fin-
est of the flowers
Be my great holiness break these shackles of my apprehension.
Feelings of my worthlessness declined to linger.
I want to see Christ in you.
The blessed Holy Spirit

Comfort Bearing

Time to come into my breaking from my past forbearance
Finding a fresh perspective, differences in the way of being
Simple comforts never known, peace of mind no longer fleeting.
No longer in a state of restless sin racking my brain with torture
Treading forth on the beaten path of life
Venturing out into the world and leaning on the Lord
Never settling for the last of breaths waiting to take another.
Looking for a comfort bearer another to share in gratitude
Let us make truthful rest, comfort, and gentle hands.
A mainstay of our lives

SECTION III

Brothers and Sisters

All of us that Glory in the Lord are like brothers and sisters
Let not your anger last lest together we fall apart.
Along with a beautiful picture of a beautiful church
Each one of us, not just a brick or binding
But the fill inside and the presence of the one true spirit
Spreading joy and love to a world fed a lie.
Making new friends to join our ends and put forth a more
prominent family
Our father is the greatest without a flaw, thus beheld.
He cares for us when we are down and lifts us up.
He protects us when we are in trouble.
For with him, no matter the outcome, we know we have a home.
Where all get-together, and we laugh, and we dance
At the high gates of Heaven rejoicing together.
Brothers and sisters, forever we are friends.

Insanity to Brevity

Dead and I am dying hurt, and I am crying.
Not knowing who I am or who I want to be
Looking out for a little bit of comfort
To ease the repetitious dissatisfaction.
Breaking my mind running and hiding do not know where to go.
Why I am fleeting and going so far away.
Never even thinking about what I could do to be better by you.
Until you struck me took and you loved me
Held me up and set me on the right path
Gave me my map and compass
The one way, the solitary truth, the light in the darkness
You teach me just who I am and what I need to do.
So that I can grow and teach others not only to keep to myself but to share
No trial nor burden
Destruction nor mindless insanity
Can take away the blessing raining down
My mind has come back to sanity.
Amen

Inter Omens

Do not look to unbury the dead.
To dig up the past when it has laid to rest.
Instead, honor the memory and the spirit of what has been
So that we all can live again
Some of us are almost there, nearing the departure of the Earth.
To you, how much have you done? Some may never know.
How often do we spend time with you as we indeed should?
To learn what there is and what has been in turn to enrich our lives.
Not only that, but to cherish what all you have done and who
you are and were
The many stories left untold people forgotten in the world.
Never should we forget all of you
It would be a shame to be cast aside.
For one day, we will all be there looking for respect.
Dignity with age is something to aspire to and to hold most dear.
For we all have elders who led us here and built upon this land
We all have family, a place where we are from
So, I ask that you take the time for them to bless sincerely.
Then you will be blessed in turn.
Amen

Wedding

Looking for a bride, a woman to get on her best side
To lead into a most fine romance.
Not a worry, but an unusual happenstance
Most beautiful in all her beauty
Dressed in the most elegant fashion
Beaming from ear to ear a grin irreplaceable
To see me there as I stand as proud as could be, happiness to match.
A woman like no other ever told.
To join all our days and speak of our great love.
Nobody can match the amazement that you bring to me.
I hope that you will have me.
To take me with you as you go.
Wherever we are, whether near or far
I will never let you go.
A bride of peace and merciful ease
Bearing all a man could want, need, and ask of
Glorious day I wait for you.
The day I become whole.

Best of Friends

You are all that I hope for in life.
The real and best of friend
An absolute and complete partner, a helpmate through and through
To teach me love again and do it better than before
Run me wild with your wonderfulness and grace
Trust me with all my strength to care and do what must be
We work together and fight for all we want
Communicate our best of wishes and try to make them true
Soft felt touch and a lover's embrace shall mark us when we meet.
Looking for all this love and more for you to add
Wanting for myself something I have never had

Run Away

Time to get away from here
To travel to a different time or place.
Going on my road to look for a lost faith
Wondering why all I can do is never enough
No matter what I try always seeming to fail
Examining my life and measuring all my memories
Seeing what was for good and what doomed from the beginning
What was noble intent, and what meant for greed?
Finding that I need to come forward and take a different leap
One of faith where I put in more reliable hands
Learn from my past and stop it from repeating
I know I am not the only one filled full of regret.
Let us all conquer our debt and pay forward to the world.
Giving till it hurts and not trying but doing what is needed

Through the Ocean

Wading through the water, dolphins passing by.
No sharks in sight but schools of fish looming and swimming fast by
To be akin to one would be an exciting find.
Swimming by and through all over the ocean
Being one of the creatures of the deep
Survival rest on a need to pass by quickly
For if you slow an easy target made
Like pray for a shark, the devil has his day.
But not for long, for he will be bound
In a different kind of lake
One of fire
Where he is undoubtedly going to burn

SECTION IV

Heartfelt

Painstaking and not forgotten nor disvalued
Chief in my eye and the bulk burden on my mind
Not a distress but a positive force keeping me going on
A heartfelt companion our fate dually held.
From one day to the next, priestess of my heart
Looking for a confidant, fellow, and a friend
Hoping for a great unison to fill this empty void
A pick me up when I am down a lift when I am weary.
I will do the same for you.
So together we can be whole.

Chilling Stare

A devilish stare, a glaring fury
Looking to take me and foment my agitation
A quick deceit, a lie-filled cover-up
A death to my deepest disguise
Hiding from the world outside taking on a false form
An anger from deep within, I hope that I can quiet.
This storm of passion, anguish, and vengeance
Deep sorrow and deathly vitriol
A brooding of a false set pride
Where my anger and my hate set to dine dually
A supper of vile, vicious deception
Dear Lord, free me from this consternation.

Never Ending

Undying ceaseless, endless pain
Looking for a new felt mind
Deeply disquieted, never can I not hear a million voices.
Looking for one that makes one that I have listened to before
A familiarity a break from this psychosis
I cannot find my mind to make any sense.
A rambling death trolls keeping me trapped inside
Please do not take me to be weaker.
For lost in this insanity
When I wake and gain my thought
I find I can be somewhat bright.
Not the least of intellect nor the most unwise
Though before the wisdom came foolishness and guise
Death nearly came many a day as I dropped all my strength.
Thinking I would be trapped in a cell and going through hell
From one day till the end of my life
Even outside of it, I am still trapped inside.
With an almost fried brain
Then I found a way out; the Lord led me through it.
Otherwise, I would not have made it with all that stood in the way.
I happy to have his presence.
That way, I can escape my vertical descent.

Waking Up

Bring me to life, fill me up and love me.
I need much more than what was in store.
Before my madness conquered and I set down a broken path
The drive to thrive was set aside, but now it is set deep.
Waking up to a brand-new feat
A call not of the wild
One instead of redemption, wonder, and filled with hope.
Cannot wait to see what is in store for me for the rest of my days
Will I be successful
Or will I fall and stumble
Not a bum any longer nor a shattered soul
With me now, I want to see you together by my side.
Where I can thrive and do more than survive
Then I can wake up more fully.

They Will not Defend You

When your broken and disconnected, torn apart and filled with shame
Do not ask for help from them; you will feel dejected.
While you are shoved with all the rubbish, the perpetrators' aim
To keep you down, punish you, and take away your pride.
They will not defend you; do not look for them to care.
They will not outlive you, so do not let yourself feel despair.
It is not the end; you can live again and be born anew.
They cannot rob you or leave your spirit barren.
The Lord will revive you and bring you up with him.
You are not alone, even though they will not defend you.
I will pray for you again every night before bed.
I had misled and hurt all the way when I was young.
Shoved to the side, I hid, and I cried the tears that nearly bled.
Always felt worthless or that I am less of a man.
Not healthy but useless could not defend myself in the end.
I thought I was tough, made hard by the fire, but I buried my soul deep.
Caught up in lies the fall, the demise the aim of the thieves of free will
I was broken and abused, so I pick up a new shield of it I will surely use
Defend my last shred of pride, pick it up and watch it grow
Because I know they will not defend me
You are not alone

Suffering King

I am a lost, torn, ripped, and broken man once a prince before a king.
Looking into the hourglass tower and finding the sand has
fallen on my reign.
It is time to suffer blood and hardship time for more false decrees again.
Things got reckless when my time ran out on me.
Taken and thrown aside like a conquered man beaten and desolate
I got diffused and sent confused into the lair of the pitted snakes.
My time ran out on me a suffering king in darkness peril is all I see
Got blasted to the chest, and the face got a death beat
rhythm following me.
I woke up in this place far from home. I know I was lost and look-
ing for some help.
But deceit was all I saw nobody to catch me as I fall.
My most disastrous fiend came to pleasure in my demise.
He said I was weak in rule and easy to conquer a leader without his army.
He beat and broke my sanity, and my spirit crushed as well.
But I am not so easy to capture and kill, not one to see the
end from defeat.
So, I wake up and clean off the blood from a battle, not foretold.
One where the ogre has drawn first blood, but his false foot-
ing is his undoing
I am not just a prodigal son but a man, a king in his time.
I lay down myself in fashion to rise again with God, for he will help
me conquer again.
Not lost too long brought to the edge of death.
But still, hell could not overcome what God has claimed for me.
He is the rock chief cornerstone, the Lord the real King to whom I bow.
He is the original suffering one who brought the cross to bear
He brought me back from nearly dead, picked me up, and
gave me a new life.
One where I am healthy again, and it is not the end the ogre is
coming to defeat

I am laying down the law with the word of God, like justice to my foe.
Back from the lair of the pitted snakes, I have got venom in my veins.
Not one to die without a fight or go down without being dragged
I wake up each day, laying down my battle plan for sure victory.
I have a cross to bear, and it is mine.
Should you like to help, join the army.
We would indeed welcome you and bring you with us to the fight to end
the dragon's reign.
It is a sword for the fallen and ice hearts of the wicked.
I have brought no truce nor vice for the shame of the fallen; they are not a
far cry from the edge.
The ogre was brought down by its shame, decried, and low-
ered to its place.
Now it is time for the decrepit deceiver, the father of lies slith-
ering one of woe.
We have got an ax to grind and mortar to spill a tethering of the chains.
Brought to the lake of fire where he is sure to be beaten
In the end, he's Godforsaken the timeless enemy since the
dawn of creation.
He has had me lost for so long, drawn-out suffering.
Ever since I was a king, I have been on his list marked for his anger.
He takes out on me and stunts my growth looking to stop
me in my tracks.
Almost buried me deep, locked me up, and drowned me in his moat.
But the dragon cannot kill what God has borne by the bearing of
his shed blood.
So, when Heaven shines its light on me, I will not let up or let down.
Just going to keep going with the barrage, a fatal attack against the snake
Hell cannot drag me down or stake; its claim to my very soul.
Because unlike the devil, I am not Godforsaken

Dead Heart Revived

Laid down to rest from a broken, shattered soul
Fallen asleep in my numbness without feel for any pain
My dead heart cannot feel anymore is bled; all it can bleed.
Jewels and fame do not sway me in my stay.
Never going to get caught in a ruthless escapade
A shadow of myself from my yesterday
Never put down the tirade of death, a loud façade, a disap-
pointing moment.
Tears do not run from me anymore; no matter how sad I get, I
have used them all.
Heart is dead; will you please revive it with your love.
I would share in your pain any day.
Do not think I am so insensitive I could not love you the same.
My victory is a smile on your pretty face.
A final beat from my heart to wake it up and end this masquerade
That I do not feel the way I think or that it is not natural to me
I wake up every morning waiting for revival; if it is all I get, I am blessed.
I wear a mask with laughs to hide my pitiful shame.
Do not know why it happened; I would fail to explain.
I just want to be loved.

Fire Borne

Take a light to a lamp and burn the oil.
Search for a way outside the cave of your pitfall
Dimly lit and unaware
Let Heaven lead you on your road.
A shadow has foretold.

His fire borne hell cannot defeat
Reclaimed by blood and flesh redeemed
Unaware and unprotected
My savior has reclaimed.

Send the storm, let it rain on me.
Spirit all aflame in his holy name
So, let his blood pour down on you.
It is not a different tired rite of truth.
Never-ending love will shelter us.
He is the way the path I am counting on
The heartache in my veins will not follow me again.
And when that shadow falls, it cannot touch you.
You have the spirit of a dove.

His fire borne hell cannot defeat
Reclaimed by blood and flesh redeemed
Unaware and unprotected
My savior has reclaimed.

We are in the summer of the eve of day.
The world cannot proclaim victory on us.
With the Holy Spirit, we cannot lose the war.
I have got an itch to see it through.
Tears will not empty me.

His fire borne hell cannot defeat
Reclaimed by blood and flesh redeemed
Unaware and unprotected
My savior has reclaimed.

No, you cannot make a fool of me at all.
Let it rain blessings from above.
Pour his spirit out on you.
We all know who we are in him.
It is in our veins, oh.
Tonight, we sing again.

His fire borne hell cannot defeat
Reclaimed by blood and flesh redeemed
Unaware and unprotected
My savior has reclaimed.

Finally

As you have heard what I have thought and where I have been
My final request is that you judge with all your kindness.
What I have had my hopes my dreams.
I fill my happiness for things in store
What I want and who I want to be
If you will see me as the Lord would have
More beautiful than I could hope
Not ugly, misshapen, and distorted
An object of curiosity or at least not a monstrosity
Perhaps a worthwhile friend.
And so, we end this tale of mine.
One of many different interests
Rest in ease and hope for peace
My prayers for you are to be undoubtedly blessed.

Outro

For this time, we spent pondering on the providence of God, love, and life
we shall indeed find reward. Looking not unto to selfishness but kindness,
caring, and concern. For not just ourselves but each other. We will build a
brighter day, a future with promises not broken but upheld. For if we look
above to the will of God, we will find a higher passage. Let us not grow
slowly but take this world by storm. Let us bend the world to its knees,
following as Christ shall lead. No longer weak and separate but bound to-
gether in one spirit. Brothers, sisters, mothers, fathers, lovers, and best of
friends. I write to you to see things through that I might find what I seek
and share with you in blessing.

In these moments, all we should think of is the blood of the great Lord.
For if it were not for the nails and the scars. Where would we be? I do not
wish to go there, so let not our ignorance show. Instead, let the Holy Spirit
bless us. For you see, we all have wandered, stumbled, and ungracefully
lost our tact. But we are being bolstered in the covenant of the blessed
blood of the Lamb. We share the burden, stand, and take our cross to
carry it to the finish.

What is our purpose, but to fulfill our God-given provision? Though we
all have different talents, gifts, callings, positions, and titles, God uses us
wherever he sees fit. Although this may not be in our comfort zone, it
might lead us far away. If he is the sole compass and bearing in our life,
then our decisions are precise. Where to go, when, who to take with,
sometimes wondering why. For we are only human, and God does know
we are not perfect. " As it is written: "There is no one righteous, not even
one; there is no one who understands; there is no one who seeks God. All
have turned away, they have together become worthless; there is no one
who does good, not even one." (Romans 3:10–12)

But we will find he had us in mind keeping in his spirit. " For you created my inmost being; you knit me together in my mother's womb. I praise you because I am fearfully and wonderfully made; your works are wonderful, I know that full well. " (Psalms 139:13–14). Let us join in this spirit keeping us all the while more merciful. For it is with the mercy of Christ, we are all delivered.

To women most beautiful it is to them I surely remind. " Two are better than one because they have a good return for their labor: If either of them falls down, one can help the other up. But pity anyone who falls and has no one to help them up. Also, if two lie down together, they will keep warm. But how can one keep warm alone? (Ecclesiastes 4:9–11) " Husbands, love your wives, just as Christ loved the church and gave himself up for her to make her holy, cleansing her by the washing with water through the word, and to present her to himself as a radiant church, without stain or wrinkle or any other blemish, but holy and blameless. (Ephesians 5:25–27)

Do not let the darkness conquer you, nor insanity or dying flesh cripple your ability to love. "Blessed is the one who perseveres under trial because, having stood the test, that person will receive the crown of life that the Lord has promised to those who love him. (James 1:12) Nothing is greater than the love of the Lord, and the darkness cannot overcome. "Your word is a lamp for my feet, a light on my path." (Psalm 119:105) Remember to stay healthy and persevere through trials and discomfort. "The name of the LORD is a fortified tower; the righteous run to it and are safe." (Proverbs 18:10)

www.ingramcontent.com/pod-product-compliance
Lightning Source LLC
Chambersburg PA
CBHW070444090426
42735CB00012B/2458